Company Come

A Play

Alec Baron

A SAMUEL FRENCH ACTING EDITION

SAMUEL FRENCH

FOUNDED 1830

SAMUELFRENCH-LONDON.CO.UK
SAMUELFRENCH.COM

CHARACTERS

Martha
Jesse, her husband
Tim, her son
Mary Lee, from the next farm

The action takes place in a remote farmhouse

Time—the present

COMPANY COME

A small, dilapidated, solitary farmhouse. Late afternoon, darkly overcast

Martha Hunterman is standing in shadow at the sink, washing up. She is humming to herself, quietly, in a voice like gravel. Sometimes she looks as if she is forty years old and sometimes as if she is seventy, depending upon how the light catches her and the expression on her face

The door opens and Jesse comes in, wiping his hands on his trousers, a cheeky grin on his face. He appears to be a farm labourer of about fifty

Martha (*surprised*) Jesse! What you doing here? Have you finished the three-sided field be now?

Jesse No, Martha, I ain't. Not yet. Not be half.

Martha Well, what, then? You weren't wanting yer tea so soon, were ye? It's not ready yet.

Jesse No—ah just felt a yearning to see me wife. There's nothing wrong in that, is there? (*With mounting passion*) Come here. Put them pots down.

Martha (*laughing*) Jesse! Me hands are all wet. Leave me be . . .

Jesse Never mind yer hands . . .

Martha Jesse! Just a minute—let me dry me hands . . .

Jesse Dry them, then, and let's you and me go in the back.

Martha What, now? Where's young Tim then?

Jesse He's behind the barn. I've give him a job'll keep him busy an hour sure.

Martha What if he come?

Jesse Well then, he come. We ain't breaking no law. Goodness sakes, woman, we been married twenty year.

Martha And you ain't changed one bit, Jesse Hunterman!

Jesse No, and not likely to, neither, Mrs Hunterman.

Martha I'm glad about that, at any rate.

Jesse Then that's all right then. No man wants a wife who loves out of duty.

Martha Afore night time! And you such a pious and believing
   man!
Jesse Religion ain't got nothing to do with the mysteries of
   marriage.
Martha Ah like that! It were Church what married us.
Jesse And that's as far as Church goes. God give you to me and
   me to you. The rest is up to us and there's no evil in it. Come
   here and sit on me lap.

*He drags her towards him, passionately. She shows no resistance,
just a show of modesty*

Martha Mind me leg! And let me get me pinny off, it's wet. (*She
   sits on his knee*) There!

   He kisses her

You're a good husband, Jesse, in spite of your appetites.
Jesse (*his voice quivering*) Because of me appetites, you mean. A
   good husband is one who has a good wife. And you're a good
   wife . . .

*They are interrupted by the door being tried. It is locked. A knock
is heard*

Martha (*somehow older, her voice deeper*) Who is it?
Mary Lee (*off, in the pleasant voice of a woman in her late thirties*)
   It's me, Mrs Hunterman, Mary Lee.
Martha Just a minute.

*Jesse retires to a chair in the dark part of the room. Martha, now
with a pronounced limp, shuffles to the door, unbolts and opens it*

   Mary Lee enters

Martha I keep it locked. You never know.
Mary Lee You do right. Now, I've got everything except the
   underwear you wanted. They don't seem to stock that kind no
   more. I tried both shops. Don't know what we're bound to do
   about that.
Martha Don't matter. I'll make do. What I got is on its way
   home but so am I. We'll go together. (*She sits at the table*)
Mary Lee Next time I go to market with Walter in the car I'll
   try there. Now. (*Emptying her basket*) Butter, milk, bacon,
   cocoa, bread, gauze bandage and aspirins. And a new half-

pint mug for your tea, to replace the one you broke. Do you like it?

Martha (*churlishly*) A white one would have done.

Mary Lee Well, this one was just as cheap. It's supposed to be a second, but I could see nothing wrong with it. It will happen be a bit jollier for you—it's got horses on it.

Martha Horses don't make tea taste better.

Mary Lee And there's your pension book, and here's what's over.

Martha Thanks.

Mary Lee What about Saturday then?

Martha I wrote a list. I'll get it for yer. (*She groans as she moves*) When ah can get up.

Mary Lee Your legs are bad today, ain't they?

Martha There's rain in store. Ah can always tell.

Mary Lee I was reading in Sunday paper about a new treatment someone's found. America I think it were. Works wonders with rheumatism, they say.

Martha I've stopped believing in miracles.

Mary Lee You mustn't give up.

Martha What is it? An operation? I'm not having no operation. Ah don't believe you can cure the flesh by cutting it open.

Mary Lee But they say this is different. Ask anybody.

Martha Ah don't *see* anybody. Nobody comes. Except you.

Mary Lee Well, you can't expect, can you. It's a bit remote, isn't it?

Martha Even me grandson. Not even *he* comes.

Mary Lee I've—I've never seen your grandson, Mrs Hunterman.

Martha No, you won't have.

Mary Lee You—never talk about him . . .

Martha Do you know, he only called me Granny once—when he was three. Must be eighteen or nineteen by now. I never seen him since.

Mary Lee Don't you hear from him? Don't he write?

Martha Not a grudging word. Not even at Christmas.

Mary Lee I'd have liked to see Tim's son, but I don't suppose I ever will, if that's how it is. Well, I'll go and start the supper for Walter. I'll bring your things round Saturday, about the same time . . .

Martha (*curtly*) Thanks.

Mary Lee 'Bye then.

Mary Lee goes out

Martha bolts the door behind her

Jesse (*quietly*) What's she got against *me*, then? She didn't even
   say hello.
Martha (*her voice unmistakeably lighter*) She couldn't have see
   you—sitting there in that chair.
Jesse God give us eyes to see, if folk would use them.
Martha She'd have said hello if she'd have see you.
Jesse Why couldn't you have say something?
Martha I never—it didn't strike me . . .
Jesse I felt such a damn fool sitting there like I was—well, in-
   visible. I'll get back to the three-sided field.
Martha I thought . . .
Jesse I'll get back to the field.
Martha Would you like a mug of tea?
Jesse I'll get back.
Martha Jesse . . .
Jesse What?
Martha I—I thought you wanted to go in the back . . .
Jesse The feeling's gone off.

   *Jesse goes out through the door. Although we saw Martha bolt
   it, the door opens for him without unbolting*

Martha Oh dear! Fancy him taking on like that! (*She giggles*)
   Blowed if I didn't forget Jesse was here when Mary Lee called.
   (*Mumbling to herself*) Ah well . . . Look at this—another make
   o' butter. (*She sniffs at it*) Smells a bit off to me, this one does.
   Couldn't see anything wrong with the mug, she says. It's
   chipped here at the bottom. I'd have much sooner had a white
   one. I was fond of that white mug. You get fond of things
   around you when you're on your own—it's about all you've
   got. Ah was very 'tached to that white mug. Still, if you can't
   shop for yoursen you mun take what people fetch. (*Pause. She
   looks out of the window*) It's getting dark already. What time is
   it? Well I'll be blowed, the darn thing's stopped again. (*She
   shakes the clock*) I ought to get me a new one. Still, what do I
   want a clock for? I get up when it's light and go to bed when

it's dark. And I get me something to eat when I'm hungry. Come to think, I'll have a couple of them rashers now, that she's brought. And some of that crumbly cheese. Why not? There's some bread and butter now, and it'll only go rotten if I don't.

Distant thunder is heard, then rain

There it comes—I knowed it would, with me leg hurting.

The door opens. Tim comes in, hesitantly. He is smartly dressed, city fashion. He looks to be in his twenties

Martha Why, Tim lad! How nice to see you!
Tim (*diffidently, uncomfortably*) Hello, Mother. I just beat the rain. It's going to be heavy.
Martha What you doing in these parts?
Tim I came to see you.
Martha 'Specially?
Tim Yes, 'specially.
Martha I am flattered! How's Elly? And Jimmy?
Tim James, Mother. He's called James. Elly won't have him called Jimmy.
Martha James then. How is he? James?
Tim He's at University now. Studying.
Martha Studying what?
Tim Er—anthropology.
Martha (*impressed*) Oh! (*There is a slight pause*) What's that?
Tim It's—you wouldn't understand.
Martha Sounds important though, anyway. You know, Tim, I ain't seen him these fifteen years.
Tim It's been difficult.
Martha You—wouldn't have a—photograph?
Tim I didn't bring any.
Martha Oh! (*There is a slight pause*) I'm just making supper. It won't be long. You must be hungry.
Tim I had something—in a café—just before I came.
Martha Your room is ready. I always keep it ready. How long will you be staying?
Tim Half-an-hour. I've got to get back.
Martha Half-an-hour! You mean to say you've come all this way just for half-an-hour?

Tim What we have to say to each other, we can say in half-an-
hour. Can't we, Mother?

Martha That's because we've grown apart. You could tell me
what's been happening, bring me up to date—and we could
talk about the old times.

Tim Let's forget about the old times!

Martha You didn't say how Elly was.

Tim I don't see Elly now. We've split. I told you, last time I was
here.

Martha Did you? I forget. So who's looking after you?

Tim I look after myself.

Martha Why don't you come back home, Tim?

Tim I can't do that, Mother.

Martha Why not? It would be company for both of us.

Tim I can't do that, Mother. You know I can't. I come when I
can.

Martha But you never stay long.

Tim That's because we run out of things to say to each other.

Martha You could get the farm working again.

Tim I can't do that, Mother.

The door is tried. It is locked. A knock is heard

Martha Who's that? I'm coming. (*She unbolts the door*)

Mary Lee enters

Mary Lee I am dopey. Your porridge oats are still here in my
basket. I thought you might need them in the morning.

Martha But it's raining. You're wet. Wait while it lets up a bit.

Mary Lee Just for a moment then—it might blow over.

Martha Would you like a cup of tea?

Mary Lee No thanks—Walter'll be in for his supper soon. Looks
like a rough night.

Martha Ah thought it were getting dark early.

Mary Lee Mrs Hunterman, when I go to market with Walter in
the car, why don't you come with us?

Martha Oh, ah couldn't do that. Ah couldn't get as far as the
road.

Mary Lee We could work out some way of getting you to the
car.

Martha What'd be the good—ah couldn't walk round the market.

Mary Lee You could sit in the car. It would be an outing for you. You haven't been outside this house ever since Tim died, have you?

The thunder rumbles closer

Martha I'd rather not—talk about that.
Mary Lee But you must.
Martha Why must I?
Mary Lee Fifteen years it is, since Tim died.
Martha I'd rather not talk about it.
Mary Lee Oh, come now! You *never* want to. You can't just bottle it up for ever. Surely by now you can talk about it. I can.
Martha You? What's it got to do with you?
Mary Lee I loved him too, you know.
Martha That was all over.
Mary Lee In what way?
Martha For you. All over.
Mary Lee You mean when he married? All right, I lost him, but that didn't stop me loving him. It wasn't over by any means. Not for me. I—I wanted him *more* after he went.
Martha That's what killed Jesse, when Tim went off with *her* like that. The doctor gave it a fancy name but *I* knew what it were. We always thought that Tim would take over the farm. Everything we did here was for him. The way we worked when he was little! That bitch! She took him away. It killed Jesse, sure as frost in winter. And there I was, left on my own. *I* couldn't farm on my own.
Mary Lee We all thought you'd get someone in to work it for you.
Martha No! Ah don't want anyone else here. Ah never did and ah don't now. They're all rusted, the machines, any road. The animals all died—I couldn't look after 'em, not after me knees started to go.
Mary Lee I'm surprised Tim didn't come back, after your husband died. It would all have been his, the farm and everything.
Martha It was *her*, if you must know. She wouldn't have it. She took him away. He wouldn't listen to me, or his father, once *she* came on to the scene.
Mary Lee Where is she now?
Martha Ah don't know.

Mary Lee And the boy?

Martha (*shouting*) Ah don't know, ah tell yer! Don't keep asking me questions. Ah don't know. You'll only upset me. (*Close to tears*) Can't you see ah don't want to talk about it?

Mary Lee All right! Bottle it up! (*Pause. She goes to the door*) Looks like the rain's set in. I'll be on my way. I'll see you Saturday.

Mary Lee goes

Martha bolts the door, then turns

Martha Ah'm sorry, Tim.

Tim Is it true, Mother?

Martha What, son?

Tim What she said? Did I die?

Martha You do ask daft questions. How could you have died? You wouldn't be here talking to me if you had, would you?

Tim I suppose not.

Martha Talk sense. Now get yourself ready—your dad'll be in soon.

Tim Father?

Martha Yes. He's been on the three-sided field. He'll be tired. It's hard work, that field. I thought you'd have helped him.

Tim When—is this, Mother?

Martha When? (*Impatiently*) Does it matter when?

Tim Is it before?

Martha Before what?

Tim Before Elly?

Martha You bet it is. Elly doesn't come into this.

Tim Did you tell the truth when Mary Lee asked, Mother? Did Elly marry again?

Martha Ah don't know nothing about Elly. Ah heard nothing from her.

Tim And James?

Martha Go and wash your hands. Supper's nearly ready.

Tim Please tell me, Mother—I'd like to know.

Martha Ah've told you everything ah know. Ah can't tell you what ah don't know, can I? Come on now, here's your father.

Jesse comes in

Jesse Ah didn't finish. Ah'll have to go back there in the morning. It's starting dark.

Martha Tim'll help you tomorrow, won't you, Tim?

Jesse Oh, is Tim here? Ah didn't see you, Tim, standing there in the shadow. Are you feeling better?

Tim Yes, Dad.

Jesse Ah missed you today. It's dark there by the sink, Martha. We did have that sink put in the wrong place, you know. It should have been here by the window, like I said.

Martha I prefer having the *table* by the window. Ah did then and ah do now. Don't you, Tim?

Tim Yes, it's better, I expect. We could do with a lamp though, by that sink.

Martha We'll get one. We'll have everything in time. It's only just about now, between light and dark when you notice it. At night, with the lamp lit, it's as light as everywhere else and during the day when the sun shines it don't matter. Get thee washed, Jesse.

Jesse Aye. (*Going to the sink*) Mary Lee rode by this afternoon on that dapple pony. Did she call here?

Martha No she didn't. *I* didn't see her.

Jesse (*washing*) Oh, she were heading this way. Thought she were looking for Tim.

Martha No... (*Lying*) Tim were in all afternoon, in the bedroom, lying down, weren't you, Tim? Yer didn't see her, did you?

Tim She *was* here, Dad. Just before you came in. She left a few minutes ago.

Jesse Ah must have just missed her.

Tim She's looking old, isn't she, Mother?

Jesse Old? Ah wouldn't have said that. Rosy cheeks, riding good as any man. Ah don't know what's the matter with you, Tim. She likes you, you know. You could have her if you wanted and you know it.

Martha Yes—and go and work their farm for 'em. That's just what her father wants, mark my words.

Jesse You're twenty-two, son—it's time you were thinking about——

Martha (*interrupting, and raising her voice*) You'll find yourself a wife who'll come and live here. With us! Ah could do with a bit of help—ah can't get around as well as ah used to. When ah went into town last time ah thought ah wasn't going to be able to get back over my knee. There's that Endersby girl from Moor End. They've got four sons and three daughters—they wouldn't miss one. *She*'d come and live here.

Jesse What's wrong with Mary Lee? She's an only child. She'll get that farm one of these days—Tim would have them both in time. Both farms. Make one *big* farm.

Martha (*sharply*) He'd get nothing from that old miser. I know him better than you. We was both brought up in these parts before you came here, Jesse Hunterman. I *know* him, too well.

Tim I wish you two would shut up and leave me be. I'll find somebody when I'm ready.

Jesse Well, if you're not ready now you never will be. I always believed in planting early.

Martha Aye, but in the right soil. Their farm gets more run down every year.

Jesse And ours gets a bit better every year, don't it, Tim? But you need a wife and family to run it properly. Nothing like your own. Your mother and me won't last forever. And don't linger too long. Every farmer knows that if you do one thing late, you'll be late with everything else.

Martha There's that dance, Saturday week, in the Hall, Tim. Why don't you go and get friendly with that Endersby girl— the chubby one with the fringe. She looks a nice one, that one. Good solid thighs. She'll do well by you.

Jesse Yes, why don't you, Tim. Mary Lee will be there, too.

Tim I'll see.

Martha Come on then, sit you down. I'll dish up.

Martha puts a piece of cheese on a plate and brings it to the table. She cuts a slice of bread and butters it. She sits at the table. Jesse and Tim also sit, but only Martha eats. Thunder rumbles

There's going to be a real'un by the looks. It's hanging. Do you think you ought to go out and close those shutters, Jesse? It's been asking for it all day, mind.

Rain starts again

There it comes.

Jesse Won't do no harm. Best rain of all, thunder rain. Penetrates deeper than anything. Loves it, the soil do. Loves being pene-trated deep. All living things do.

Martha Now, Jesse.

Jesse Law of nature. Law of all living things. And soil's a living thing. The life of the soil goes into the seed, and into the man what plants the seed. Livingest thing of all if you ask me, the ground.

Thunder

Martha There ain't *no* dead things. Everything's living. The sky's living.

Tim Don't be daft, Ma.

Martha Just *listen* to it! You can't call it not living when it makes itself heard like that. *And* it brings forth its fruit like all living things.

Tim Fruit? The sky?

Martha You bet it do. Everything in its season. The sunshine and the rain. And the snow. They all come out of the sky. And where would we be without the sunshine and the rain? Dying of thirst and hunger, in the dark.

Tim Everything can't be living, Ma.

Martha It is, I tell you. Ain't it, Jesse?

Tim What about them folk up there on the hill, under those great heavy stones? They're dead, ain't they?

Martha Depends. They lived, and they were warmed by the sun, and they brought forth their fruit like everything in nature.

Tim But they're dead now. Good and dead.

Martha Some of them are and some of them aren't. They live on as long as there's someone to remember 'em. As long as there's a picture in someone's album to look at, they're not dead.

Tim What about them before there was cameras? What about them? They're not in any albums.

Martha There's all kind of ways. Don't you see? Words! Right from the beginning of time. Those people in the Bible—they live on, don't they? For ever. And those what wrote it—they live in those words. They're more alive now than they ever was —all over the world—they're living all right.

Tim Lot's of folk never had any words written about 'em. Plain folk, what never done nothing worth remembering.

Jesse There's different ways of remembering, son. A tree can live a long time, and then die, and you might think there's no-one to remember it. But its seeds made other trees, sturdy young trees, and where would they have been without it? It lives on in them. They might not remember, the way we can remember—we don't know that, do we?—but as long as there's someone or something following on, as long as there's something in somebody's mind they're alive all right.

Martha Your father's right, Tim. That's why you're here.

Thunder

Tim (*laughing*) All my grandfathers and my grandmothers then —if I call 'em to mind now, they're here. Right?

Martha That's right, son. Call 'em to mind and they're back here. With us.

Tim Good job we don't have to feed 'em.

They all laugh. It becomes a jolly scene, in no way morbid. They are all having fun

Jesse Ah wouldn't mind feeding 'em, all the blooming lot of 'em, if they'd do a fair day's work on the farm.

Martha If they do no work, they don't get fed.

Tim They can sit at the table then, but not eat.

Jesse Your old uncle—'Lijah—I call him to mind, so he's here!

Martha Oh, not him!

Jesse Hello, 'Lijah, you old lecher. Hey, you mind the time, Martha, when 'Lijah and that . . .

Martha Not now, Jesse. Not when we're eating . . .

Tim Why? What did he do, Dad? You never told me about 'Lijah, Ma.

Martha gives Jesse a look

Jesse Another time, Tim. Remind me—I'll tell you about 'Lijah.

Tim Did I know him, Ma?

Martha No, thanks be.

Tim Why thanks be?

Martha All he ever brought to our family was shame. That's what Parson said. (*Unexpectedly she begins to laugh*)

Jesse And fun! He were the jolliest man in your family, Martha, even though he were a dirty old bugger.

Martha Your cousin Lottie were no better.

Tim Who was Lottie? You never spoke of no Lottie.

Martha No, not when you were there, we didn't.

Jesse She were fond of men, Lottie was. Very fond. Right from being a young 'en. Liked to show what she'd got, and she had plenty. Too much sap, she had, as well. Born with it. Finished up a prostitute in Manchester, she did. Five shillings a time is what we heard.

Martha And that were too much! A deal too much!

Jesse (*hardly able to talk for laughing*) It's a good job—it's a good job she never came up agin your 'Lijah. The ground would have shook.

Tim Well, you've called her to mind—so according to you she's here with us. Hello, Lottie lass, come on in. Where are you? I say, Dad, can you lend me five bob?

Martha You'll get a sight more than your five bob's worth, like as not, same as 'Lijah did.

Jesse And that's no picnic, *I* can tell you.

Martha *You* can tell him? How can *you* tell him?

Jesse He told us—'Lijah did. All the gruesome details. We nearly pee'd oursens with laughing. You'd never *believe* what they do to you.

Tim What do they do, Dad? Tell us.

Martha (*laughing*) Don't you dare. Do you hear?

A car is heard driving up and stopping

Jesse Why not? We're all grown up . . .

Martha listens. Thunder

Martha It's that damned Mary Lee again. There's no peace from that woman.

There is a knock at the door

Mary Lee (*off*) It's me—Mary Lee.

Martha What are *you* doing here again? In this?

Mary Lee Open the door.

Martha Just a minute. Ah'm coming. (*She unbolts the door*)

    Mary Lee comes in

Mary Lee Walter brought me, in the jeep—he's waiting for me. We've been to see to the cattle.

Martha Oh.

During the scene which follows, Tim and Jesse remain seated by the table, listening

Mary Lee I couldn't rest thinking of you here by yourself in this.
Martha I'm not a baby.
Mary Lee I thought I'd just come over and close the shutters from outside—but I heard you crying.
Martha Ah weren't crying. Ah were laughing.
Mary Lee (*looking at her strangely*) Laughing? By yourself?
Martha There's no law.
Mary Lee I'll—I'll go and close the shutters.
Martha (*resentful at being disturbed*) Ah'd rather you didn't. They'll only need opening again tomorrow. Ah'd rather have the morning light, whatever the weather. Thanks just the same, but you needn't have bothered. You shouldn't come out in this.
Mary Lee I thought you'd be lonely—frightened maybe . . .
Martha Ah'm used to being by myself. Ah've learned how to manage. Ah know how to occupy my mind. And I don't frighten easily—not any more. So you can go about your business and don't worry about me.
Mary Lee (*finally stung into outspokenness*) You don't like me, do you? You never have. No matter what I do.
Martha (*unconvincingly*) Yes, I like you. You're very good to me. Ah don't know what ah'd do if it weren't for you.
Mary Lee You always had something against me. It was you who stopped Tim marrying me, wasn't it? He told me.
Martha That's a lot of poppycock.
Mary Lee Why were you agin it?
Martha Ah weren't agin nothing.
Mary Lee It was because my father turned *you* down, wasn't it?
Martha (*over-reacting*) How d'yer mean?
Mary Lee When you asked him if he'd marry you.
Martha Ah never asked him nothing. I never spoke to your father.
Mary Lee No, not after. (*Rubbing it in*) But you begged him, didn't you? You begged him to marry you.
Martha Ah never spoke to your father.
Mary Lee No, not after he turned you down and married my mother.
Martha Ah don't know where you get ideas like that. You've got a good imagination.
Mary Lee Father *told* me, afore he died. It explained a lot of

things for me. That's why you made Tim turn *me* down, wasn't it? To get your own back.

Martha Rubbish!

Mary Lee *I'm* not ashamed of telling. I asked Tim to marry me.

Martha Ah know, don't worry, he told me. Ah wish he would have married you, instead of that bitch that took him away from us. He might have been alive today 'stead of going and getting killed like that. He wasn't used to the city.

Mary Lee If he would have been with me that night at the dance he'd never have met her. She was only visiting her cousin. She wasn't one of us.

Martha It don't do to mix. Not with city folk. It don't work out.

Mary Lee He wanted me, Tim did. I know he did. Only he didn't want to go agin you. You wanted him to marry Kate Endersby from Moor End, didn't you? He told me that as well.

Martha Well, if I did he didn't take notice of me, did he? He suited himself. The darn great fool!

Mary Lee He got out, that's what he did. Away from you. He couldn't go agin you and stay. He got out.

Martha It were *her*. That damned Elly. She 'ticed him away. Lord knows what she put in them letters. Tim wouldn't tell, but ah can guess. She 'ticed him away.

Mary Lee You *drove* him away. Elly wouldn't have stood a chance on her own. *You* drove him away. I blame you, not her.

Martha (*tight-lipped*) Yes, well, don't let me keep you. Walter's waiting for you.

Mary Lee I'll go then. You're sure you'll be all right?

Martha If ah'm not used to being on my own by now ah never will be.

Mary Lee Good night then. I'd go straight to bed if I were you.

There is another rumble of thunder, more distant now

Are you sure you don't want me to close the shutters?

Martha (*unkindly*) No, thanks. Ah told you.

Mary Lee All right.

Mary Lee goes

Martha bolts the door. The car drives away

Martha Ah like that! *I* drove him away! No mother ever wanted

her son to stay more than I did. Drove him away! She doesn't
know what she's talking about. Just because he didn't want *her*
it's gone to her head.

Jesse (*slowly, quietly*) What Mary Lee said, Tim—about you
going away—is that true?

Martha No, it's not!

Jesse Ah'm asking Tim.

Tim Asking me what, Dad?

Jesse Why *did* you go? Was it because your mother drove you
away?

Martha (*loudly, angrily*) Now why should ah drive him away
when ah wanted him to stay more than anything in the world?
We only have one son—why should ah want to drive him
away?

Jesse Is it true, Tim—what Mary Lee said—is that why you went?

Tim I went—because I wanted to—marry Elly.

Martha (*shouting*) You see? Are you satisfied? It's like ah said,
she 'ticed him away. Let's have done now. No more.

Tim (*suddenly shouting back*) You can't shut him up like that!
You bring us here! Then let us speak! What do you bring us
here for?

Martha Ah bring you here because—well, because . . .

Jesse (*quietly*) She brings us here because she's lonely, son. She
brings us here to cheer her up a bit. Don't you, Martha?

Martha cries, quietly

Martha Don't you understand?—You're my life—you two—
you're what I've got. I—well, I try to—you know—(*she cries*)—
just the best parts—and there aren't so many of those—there'd
have been more if ah'd have had some sense, but ah hadn't
and there it is. You trouble me sometimes though—make me
wonder if all that went wrong were *my* fault . . .

Tim I'm sorry, Mother . . .

Martha (*trying to be cheerful, through her tears*) That's all right,
son. Come on now. It's time for bed. You'll stay, won't you,
Tim?

Tim Well I . . .

Martha Just this once—for my sake . . .

Tim All right, then—but you go to bed. I want to stay up a
while.

Martha Your dad and me'll tell you about our 'Lijah and their Lottie another time, won't we, Jesse?

Jesse Sure we will. (*He starts to giggle*) 'Specially about that time when 'Lijah and Mester Harland's wife set the haystack on fire with a cigarette . . .

Martha Now then, Jesse . . .

Jesse And they ran off, leaving his trousers and things, and all her things, to burn—

Martha (*giggling in spite of herself*) Jesse . . .

Jesse —it were funny when we all came running and there they were, looking like the day they were born, standing there like Adam and Eve just turned out of Paradise.

Martha That'll do now, Jesse.

Jesse She had two beautiful black eyes next day—and a limp— and Mester Harland never showed himself in the pub for a six-month—and I had to lend 'Lijah a pair of my trousers— those were the only pair he had, that got burnt. She were worse than our Lottie, Mester Harland's wife was—she did it for nowt.

Martha Right then, Jesse—are we going to bed?

Jesse Aye—if you don't want to talk no more. There's nothing to sit up for. It's a cold night.

Martha I'll warm you.

Jesse Yes. You're good at that, Martha. Better than any hot water bottle. Ah have to admit you're good at that. Best reason for getting wed, Tim. Mark my words. Come on, Martha.

Jesse exits to the bedroom

Martha I'm coming, Jesse. I'm coming. I'm coming . . .

Thunder rumbles in the distance, as—

the CURTAIN *falls*

FURNITURE AND PROPERTY LIST

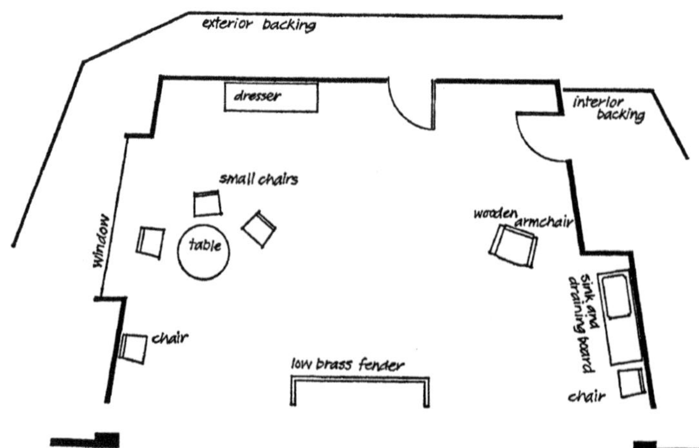

On stage: Kitchen table. *On it:* cloth, bread on board with knife, butter in dish, plate, knife, cup, saucer
5 small chairs
1 wooden armchair
Dresser. *On it:* cheese in dish with knife, clock, oil lamp, crockery, etc. as dressing
Sink (practical). *In it:* bowl with dirty dishes. *On draining-board:* mop, soap, various kitchen utensils. *On rack:* towel, cloth
Low brass fender (indicating range)
Window curtains and outside shutters
Trick bolt on outer door

Off stage: Basket. *In it:* butter, milk, bacon, cocoa, bread, gauze bandage, aspirins, tea mug, porridge oats **(Mary Lee)**

LIGHTING PLOT

Property fittings required: oil lamp (dressing only)
Farmhouse room

To open: General effect of overcast, threatening, shadowy afternoon
No cues

EFFECTS PLOT

MADE AND PRINTED IN GREAT BRITAIN BY
LATIMER TREND & COMPANY LTD PLYMOUTH

MADE IN ENGLAND

www.ingramcontent.com/pod-product-compliance
Ingram Content Group UK Ltd.
Pitfield, Milton Keynes, MK11 3LW, UK
UKHW021819150726
7214IPUK00017B/203